WHAT BOOKS PRESS

AN IMPRINT OF

THE GLASS TABLE

COLLECTIVE

LOS ANGELES

ALSO BY JAN WESLEY

Living in Freefall
A Closeness of Vision
Running Out of Altitude

ONLY SO MUCH

ONLY SO MUCH

POEMS

JAN WESLEY

LOS ANGELES

Copyright © 2022 by Jan Wesley. All rights reserved.
Published in the United States by What Books Press,
the imprint of the Glass Table Collective, Los Angeles.

Library of Congress Cataloging-in-Publication Data

Names: Wesley, Jan, author.
Title: Only so much : poems / Jan Wesley.
Description: Los Angeles : What Books Press, 2022. | Summary: "Memories of a woman seeking change and forgiveness. The narrator and characters who speak for her unravel adventures and consequences over the course of decades"-- Provided by publisher.
Identifiers: LCCN 2022020937 | ISBN 9781733378932 (trade paperback)
Subjects: LCGFT: Poetry.
Classification: LCC PS3623.E779 O55 2022 | DDC 811/.6--dc23/eng/20220502
LC record available at https://lccn.loc.gov/2022020937

Cover art: Gronk, *Untitled*, mixed media on paper, 2021
Book design by Ash Good, www.ashgood.com
Author photo: Wayne Shimabukuro

What Books Press
363 South Topanga Canyon Boulevard
Topanga, CA 90290

WHATBOOKSPRESS.COM

to
the Davids

POEMS

SECTION ONE
The Art of Memory	7
Monday Monday	8
Don't Wait Up	10
Stalking Memory at a Hotel by the Beach	12
Marking Up the Earth	14
Invisible	15
Los Angeles	17
Under the Influence	19
A Day in the 100's	21
that lingering need for ritual	23
Her	24

SECTION TWO
Day One	29
Sitting Pretty in Suburbia	31
Learning About Men	32
Inner Ear	33
Nothing Tied Down	34
Working On a Movie in My Old Hometown	35
Taking Cover	36
Whispers and Vows	38
Elegy One: Letting Go	40
Great Escapes	41
Pettable Wallpaper	42
Elegy Two: Knowing	43

SECTION THREE

The Davids	47
Prescriptive Fiction	49
A Day Off	51
Bleed	53
Flight #505	54
Car Wars	58
Swimming with Homeless Men Who Sleep Beneath the Pier	60
Calling in Gone	62
Rough Trade	63
Only So Much	65

SECTION FOUR

The Retrieval: Airport: Day	69
History Repeats Itself, Repeats Itself	70
1968	72
Alone in the Storm	73
Cautionary Tale	74
Lying On the Floor and Lying to Oneself Are Equal in Stature	75
Come On and Take It	76
Love Fallen to the Ground	78
The Future	80
Climbing Out of Quarantine One Limb at a Time	81
Acknowledgements	83
Notes	84

I think we are well advised to keep on nodding terms with the people we used to be, whether we find them attractive company or not. Otherwise they . . . come hammering on the mind's door at 4 AM . . . and demand to know who deserted them, who betrayed them, who is going to make amends.

Elizabeth Hardwick

All of the awakenings, or the old unconscious lies . . .

David St. John

SECTION ONE

THE ART OF MEMORY

There is a book inside my head of what I can and cannot do and now the light handles me like water—too much/not enough and a year disappears like rabbits back into a hat. The day is a bath of calm, gentle push against the skin, somewhere the stain of midnight oil, the linger and instinct to archive this life into tidy pyres.

Adrenaline was my first drug and I loved leaps from balconies, thrills of corporal flight, of slippery ice, the chase. Inside the house mother taught me art and solitude, hanging over drawings I made with people's hair ablaze and arms flailing with glory. Soon I got loose with my affections, learning not to touch a man where it hurt too much, alert for threat, ambush tough to see coming when first car blows a gasket, small animals get nabbed from the yard, and one day at school a boy named Steven lands his leather shoe into my chest, mother mending broken skin after the fight.

Some days memory arrives like pepper spray in the face or some days it wanders like silver writing across the sky—white girls lying in the sun until thin fair skin turned dark in a racist town, precision-built souffles dropped from my sophisticated mother's grip. Sometimes I step out of the tub and behind my eyes a doll's head drops through a grate, fifth grade boy gets misdiagnosed and dies, first black skirt scrapes my thighs as I walk to a favorite uncle's funeral. Tonight the mind shuts down like hibiscus in the dark, Sunday slathering a balm across remembrance as I close the book, liberate myself from memory's sleight of hand that keeps nesting up my sleeve.

MONDAY MONDAY

Last night she dreamed
of miscreant men who cheat
and steal and leave like a season,
silent letter from her mother's
hand open on the table, pretty paper
damaged and she reads, eats
a scone until the mother's words

create alarm of potential injury.
Red engine truck horns shriek
outside as neighbors lean from open
doors stepping tender-footed
and frightened it will be *them*
this time to flee the surprise of fire.

She swoops up the *Times* to scan
bold headlines of war—63
bodies by the road in Kabul—murder
murder, no answer, no mercy
in sight. Railings contain garden
weeds that demand extraction,
and street chatter fades

as the faint un-whine of sirens
assures a cluster of neighbors
they are free from the flames
of danger. She locks the door, checks
smoke alarms and slams
on her brake where a knife-edged
swerve sends a spiffy man in a dream
car inches off her backside
bumper as he flips her the bird. By nine,

office workers hunker down
in a borough of cubicles fashioned
in plywood furniture ensembles
keeping time with ubiquitous clicks
on computer keys without having
to look at what the messages make.

DON'T WAIT UP

First is your long-calved leg as it finds a way
from under padded cover and a peek of hair

flits through muzzled light, a binge of fingers
working like a wound to seek tenderness

and comfort. I forget how journeys back to work
remind me of days away, chasing memory

of Monterey Bay in 2012, feeding fish to seals
with your children, eating lobster on Baja sand.

Your other leg drops away from the bed, my face
in dizzy wakefulness for you as I fondle

your skin, its golden hues from ranch sun,
a neighbor's motor bike slipping gears as it sails

into hilly dry horizons. The malady of morning
news is lifted from asphalt and we could never live

in this silence, every stumble from davenport
to the bed pawing at the pelvis and both of us

grazing each other with our hands for balance.
Birds at the window mock our song as you

ask which freeway I'll take, crawling up and off
your confident abdomen until soon we notice

how seeds of the living have bloomed overnight,
ashamed we argued until dawn, invisible now

to the wrath we felt, so we leave it at that. I drive
to Malibu to screen the movie for producers who

want to check the sex scenes, blindsides of violence,
to go back and forth and back and forth for hours

to find surety and peace that audiences will weep
when man meets woman, stranger kills everyone.

STALKING MEMORY AT A HOTEL BY THE BEACH

Hollywood producers in the lobby with living
bamboo and wall to wall rattan sofas

make deals over pricey scotch, pitch movie script
fiction to bevvies of boys in bold Italian ties.

Sultry wives smoke thin cigars, decide whose husband
is top dog CEO, flies in private jets, has the longest

portfolio. Fashion models chomp at the bit and jeweled
bags bang against flat-lined bones like screen doors.

I rise, invisible to escape through a slalom course
of tables on a patio covered in twosomes

bonded over brandy and tiramisu. I shuck
my shoes to kick through sand and dampness

along the hotel's seaside wall of windows, darkness
thick as it always was when we buckled

beneath a sky chattering in astral glow. Phosphorous
laced ocean waves claw my feet as I wade

knee-deep into water that flanks the coast
of West L.A. with nothing visible in suites but sway

of silhouettes stripping for sex. I know you stayed here
weeks ago, your sensate mouth sipping tea

in this accidental coastal town, our year after college
in a one-bedroom shack, pawing at the future, soaked

in rejection slips, desire under galaxies, my surrender
to wanting you, wanting you and howling at the moon.

MARKING UP THE EARTH

I loved the way we'd mark ourselves up on shorelines by the sea, sand etching stains of grains into our flesh. Morning solar majesty stripes the sky over fields of weeds and billows of water, crowns of dewy trees, birds alert, talons dug into the bark. We wake with creases that sleeping deeper than a doze can make, our first touch of flesh denting the sheets.

In the days of our youth, we flung ourselves from rooftop launch pads, sticking gymnastic landings, rolling into accidental gropes, and later notches of lust nicked up our knees as signs of sex on carpets, on the green grass behind stadium walls.

I never got tattooed, not even drunk or under sway of men who inked *forever* like it honored the name of a favorite car, but if I etched my skin I would want to say, *remain brave*. When my mother died, her face was scarred by alcohol and electrified mental treatments of dubious cure, and I plunged into grief, into the flesh with a needle tip smaller than a citrus seed to suffocate the shock.

Marks of age, stabs of desperate measures emboss the body the way creatures find food beneath the ground, and I tell you this as we track through the yard, poking holes into the earth where tomato plants and fuchsias go, our paint penetrating canvas.

INVISIBLE

A bus stop shades her under a canopy and lamp post
at an intersection of boulevards where the woman

sits barely visible on the fringe of nose-to-bumper
cars, her child's backpack propped against her knees.

She beckons her boy to the bench and holds him
close to her like food in a famine, dismissing hunger

and adorned in cascade of hair, a line of flowers
ringing the hem of her dress. I watch from my idling

car at the light on a blind corner below balanced
well-groomed homes on the hill, and inside the shiny

machines fingers dribble keys of phones, dashboards
blinking fuel consumption, dangerous brittle brush

showing the time of day from a swipe of shadows
delivered by the sun. Her Spanish asks her child

if he can name birds pecking abandoned food as he
draws the form of a parrot with a stick. The mother

thinks of Mexico, can see abundance in the mango
groves, relatives scrutinizing news from the border

where families like her own are herded into custody,
detained like creatures in cages. There is rush of the bus

engine and she stands, looks down the block, signals
her son to her as he fiddles in the dirt, her weary body

curved from cleaning other people's homes, invisible
to drivers as the light turns green and the boy rises, opens

her fist toward the sky to pour a funnel of glistening stones
into her palm, a gift of jewels from the streets of America.

LOS ANGELES

Beside the pool
the mobile device lies under a paw
of the hyphenate-bred dog splayed flat on the cement

and after reading Variety
over lattes, I make a basketball shot
of depressing news tossed with melon rind, my mopey

Labradoodle locked in. I fly
by appliance-clothing-grocery
stores past school kids, backpacks, skateboarders waiting

for a ride and after
my driver's window opens
to the studio guard, he waves me through the iron gate

and I park in my slotted
space with no name and *how-zit
going* is first exchange with the film producer ejected

from his Porsche,
and I say *fine*, and he asks, *how's
the film?* his face in mine, beard like steel wool so I say

*all looks good but Brad
went back to the lab—his skin
is tinted green*—producer says, *print it again,* and slants

into me and I say
done, both of us quickly away
as my throat closes, same as it always does, suffocation

like the squeeze
of the ingenue's scarf around
her neck, our voices strangled, and the day has just begun.

UNDER THE INFLUENCE

The cat licks my hand and I don't know why
he loves it except perhaps rehearsal
for his own tongue's cleanse, to gather up
the taste of who protects him.

More overcast days flop out like a stain
and I think about empty gas tank
and pre-made food overstocked at the store

where boys I might have taken down
a wayward path put bags in my car. Next

door the pharmacy stocks pills
to ravage pain, bandages for things unwilling
to heal. Squirrels crawl through a bird's trampled

breakfast to pilfer seeds grown inside enormous
yellow blooms that stand shoulder to shoulder
in one of nature's displays

of beauty despite what humans can do to it.
I forget to flip the eggs and ruminate
on the shock of 1st year high school

with a new class of girls—
private school—neatly creased uniform
strides, wads of money and cigarettes

in pricey bags. Nothing was how it had been,
my Achilles heel slit open, grasp of math
and frog dissection like splintered wood in my hands.

The cat purrs a mantra and I drop a slice of health
bread into a slot to alchemize it into toast. The science

report on NPR news details how replacement
of human beings has made us drunk
on robots. Tells us we are depleted, *depleted of awe.*

I am going to change my life.

A DAY IN THE 100'S

My she doctor says get out of that
chair you slave to and shift
those green eyes away from the screen
and I do as I rise from black
swivel seat in front of the World
Wide Web and think, yes, the afternoon
sun shivers in fantastic flames. I am
exonerated and flee the house
on the hill that will topple
if someday we get too much rain. Slipped
behind the wheel of a Japanese
car clobbered with tariffs and dents
made by other flying-open doors
my foot depresses a pedal that angles
the day onto asphalt
and a few miles away
from the house I *stand on it*, high
speed acceleration into rural
farms a hundred miles out
of the city and stripe the sky with my own
jet trail as towns become hamlets. Heat
climbs all over itself to a hundred
climate-changing degrees, rebellious
light washing the fields in gold
and somewhere soy and wheat struggle
to compete with onions and lettuce,
artichokes, ripe-ready grape vines. Deep
throated theories rumble from the radio
stating the obvious about criminal

intent, and since I refuse
to listen to a president's bully
pulpit I change to classic rock, the Stones,
Stone Ponies, then jazz it up
with Coltrane and hundreds of notes
from Miles. Last night I sat in the spaceship
concert hall as a woman with whip
-like baton raised her forearms
to the orchestra and forced us to open
the body and inhale music that carried me far
from war and congeries of opiated
traffic. Insects click onto the windshield
as I feel the mile markers and trees stutter by
at a hundred miles per hour leaving
oscillations of air above asphalt,
cow herds hovered over grass
and in my wake the urban empire
has disappeared, the mind
released from civilization's frantic fits
and by noon the engine
decelerates to a windless sail as I glide
to a stop and wait for a quiet trail
of turtles to stroll across the road, home
on their backs and winking
shimmer off their incandescent shells.

THAT LINGERING NEED FOR RITUAL

Back then, as we say these days of *those* days the world was open, revolving, the body in masterful form when a stretch of tendons attached to solid bones could get me to another family holiday. Garden sprouts hid in single seeds and corners of the earth peeled back to reveal science like small animals studied in careful hands. Soon the century changed, and we lost sense of the risk of uncalculated danger the way a child might mangle fingers in a toy. We lose sight of forests and the land is laden with theft and short breath behind the throat, no end to strip-mined streets where someone's dinner lies tilted in the garbage. This holiday of thanks comes with excess food, frozen streams of cars loaded with ritual offerings, the leaves on trees turning red, yellow and dropping when they're through. I don't get soothed by turkey or lulled by tryptophan, the armor of football on tv unable to protect us anymore from family silence and squabble, and we collapse into drunkenness expecting to be forgiven once again. I ramble off somewhere between dessert and sleep to a steamy motel by the beach and a man lazes on the chilly sand. Like a habit we slide a card to enter a room, the smell of him leading me to our brief reunion. I know this kind of escape is cliché, but when my mother took her life I couldn't find solace in family commiseration and reasoning, so I found men who expected nothing except flesh and lusty animal sounds, a frenzy of the body being hushed and calmed by whispers of a stranger. He and I lean in the doorway and the moon shapes itself into a half dome along the horizon, our hands resting on tapped-out stomachs, our heads fallen back to breathe in a hundred thousand stars a minute.

HER

She and I push around the track with a shift
        in our hips, a sidestep avoiding runners

spurred by need to save themselves, to
        weed out toxins, the gnawing pace of age.

Her hair is pinned and shirt sleeves rolled
        above bug bites, a tiny line from the sun.

As if life were merely several years ago
        we remember my unglamorous sofa, fingers

tracing seams of hacked-off jeans, perfect vision
        focused on dime-sized holes in the rug,

certainties adrift, and yes, good news, sudden
        delight she carries the first child to be born

and here we settle on a bench with the years
        we've built, low-heeled shoes toeing the soil.

Seasonal rage of blooms smells like kitchens
        of our mothers, our hands limp on metallic

lace of the bench and in a lull of monotones
        we speak like hustlers of how we birthed

the slippery slopes of success and the hours give in
		to darkness, its supple cover, a dusty flick

of bugs again from crimson skin, a rise
		in her as we uncurl from the bench, decide

on salmon at her house, all the men gone, a ramble
		and moxie in us like we are young again.

SECTION TWO

DAY ONE

The nurses whisper how the father was
asleep yet he stands by the worn-out mother

with the milky food and arms of the nurse
lift me, relieve me from compression

in that birth canal, its endless quiet, and why
we struggle so, and so terribly soon, is a mystery.

Mother—she must be—stares without a glance
away, her grin, her willowy hands strong

and what I yearn for as she smooths the hair
into a cap on my head. Burps of uncharted delight

can't predict how we will flourish, how sickly
the moods will come to mangle the family one day.

A person's finger to the chin is a springboard
to kindness and they say this is memory shifting

and I never knew the mouth could work itself
and chew the air, the father's eyes sky blue,

my first lesson in color. In eighty years
the father will perish, the mother's agonies grown

like fescue flowing from the garden, a harsh
world quick to pity, to break her. These are voices

that were whispered to the mother's belly, the alto
being hers, the loud music of vocabulary his.

I see I will get more of his words, like *justice*
and *vigilance*, *history* and *art* and *remember*,

as they hand me over, tell me my name, sunlight
changing what I can see in the room. The shape

of a breast comes to my mouth, no longer being
fed alone in the dark, and feet wriggle with freedom

like the first chilly shiver from my mother's touch
as it rushes like water over the skin of my new face.

SITTING PRETTY IN SUBURBIA

A birthright to solitude sent me to sunken ditches, turtles, rabbits, slow dopey possums who nosed around the neighborhood as if everything belonged to them. Quick sprints sprung me from narrow hallways in a brick house to beautiful ruckus up and down less-traveled streets, and the boys ran me full throttle into the woods drilled by rambling paths, sun rays like rain through elms and oaks, birch trees sporting white spotted trunks that became our canvas for names carved inside hearts when kissing and fumbling touch seemed like love. At sunset mothers sang into twilight with operatic orders to get our butts home for dinners that varied in edible possibility, my mother wringing her hands around laundry, tossing liquor bottles underneath damp clothes in a basket she carried to the line. Routine was a slide through dinner, homework, no tv, reading by flashlight until sleep, until cereal, until confessing what I had done, weekends with a sack of snacks, feet like compass needles pointed toward nature's canopy, ponytail whipping my neck. The mind grew a phantom limb to believe in nothing but goodness in a future that could change situations just like that, every day a new devotion to pry addiction from mother's clutch, everything wrecked and teetering on the edge. I drew my own maps and still the ground underneath switched directions, bad decision here, worse decision there, relief from unsullied days as we'd be saved by caves and quarries, the battery of roads taking us out of suburbia where everything belonged to us.

LEARNING ABOUT MEN

We hike until the woods get thick, draped in canteens of beer that swing to a cadence we stride to and the devil girls speak in a stench of coded language. I stray ten paces behind as they mark up the earth, feet dragging leaves as light fades into the shadows, as we become one with a rustling of ghosts, sinking our bravado to whisper.

Towers of trees end at a quarry streaked in slate, the rocky floor a hundred feet below with no one to find us if we sail beyond safety, stumble to the drop. Silhouettes perch along the edge, one young boy for every devil girl, an extra guy leaning on a boulder in the shade. The girls knock back sips of beer and offer the surly boys a gulp, slaps of fear cinching my sense and courage. I murmur the alphabet backwards, certain my mother is drunk and asleep in mid-afternoon, that the girls might push those boys into the ravine, that my eyes will never close and my hair will burst into fire.

What I didn't know was how you would seduce me years later with a merciless ache of desire, how my skirt would drop around my feet, jacket whisked above my head, the body unbuttoned, unzipped, a yield of hipbones into wrap and flex of us twined against a stone wall, our skin damp from thirsty leaves of deep green ivy.

INNER EAR

> *I saw the whole piece immediately before my eyes and only needed to write it down, as though it were being dictated to me.*
>
> —Gustav Mahler referring to his symphony #8

My father made me listen to Mahler. I was ten and he was eternally in love with classical composers, especially the ones who wrote as if every concerto or symphony would be their last, might even save the world. An uncle in the Navy—electronics wizard married to my mother's sister and always silent about what he did—built my father a mono record player and speakers that today could blast hip-hop and Led Zeppelin like the best equipment designed to whirl us through space. When mother was out of the house shopping, perhaps finding liquor or selling her cameras to buy it—surreptitiously and with grief in her heart—my father would put on jazz or Mahler and crank up the volume until the whole neighborhood resounded like a concert hall. I loved how different he was from other parents—Eisenhower voters and war boosters even in the Vietnam years when 3000 Pennsylvania boys died with ears ringing from Howitzer fire and grenades. On occasion my father would play Rachmaninoff for herculean complexity and speed, remembrance of visceral passages of Concerto #2 when his own father took him to see Rachmaninoff play Rachmaninoff at Carnegie Hall. And sometimes I wish I'd been with my father before I was born—for the music—for Ella, Art Tatum, Gillespie and Monk. Tonight I sit in a seat so high above the music center's stage I'm afraid I could pitch over the railing but I don't. Instead both movements of Mahler's 8th symphony overwhelm my body with 200 voices, concentric layers of strings, timpani, tubas and horns, crescendos so grand I boil over with what magnitude can do, with what *we* can do when we are guided by another person's hand, when we listen and surrender, when we love this life enough.

NOTHING TIED DOWN

After the arguments, my mother would change how she moved, hands limp by her sides, head lowered to the cross of her legs, neck swooped like a swan's. Swabs of evening sky swept through the woods along the house while I placed utensils on cloth mats of the dinner table, unclipped a field of laundry and tilted my ear toward my parent's fight. One night, mother planted me in the car, father dimming in the driveway, tools and boxed-up remnants of our lives lost behind the garage door as we sped off and bolted down the interstate to Maryland where her sister took us in. Perhaps we stayed overnight, perhaps it rained and in the glisten of morning sun I slept all the way back home.

Tonight, the mind fights sleep with flashes of fire in the canyon as I ache for mother's zeal of being uprooted and I wonder what to take if the fire leaps the ravine. Television in the room spits evacuation orders as I pack up mother's letters to me before she died. Newscasters hesitate in the following hours and so it seems we've been spared by wind direction, erasure of nature confined to unhoused acres of hillside grass. The smoke will linger for days, September's dried sticks scuttling across the road like the sound of fingernails dragged along a desk, maple leaves sending messages from my mother, reminders *not to argue with my father, to turn off the stove. Remember to be home soon.*

WORKING ON A MOVIE IN MY OLD HOMETOWN

In Pennsylvania the war-resistant Amish ride shoulders
of the roadways with buggy wheels churning up dust.

There is hush-hush in the farmland stamped by red
barns where capped young girls look to the carriage
floorboards in plain bibbed dresses. In dazzling sunsets

they capture stray sheep and move inside their towns
with basic tools practicing traditions of forgiveness.
The Pennsylvania fields of rolling green float the body

relieve the mind and sculpt the land like dunes. Tonight
a troupe of set designers, camera pros, luminosity

wizards raise ladders above paper-thin walls to hang
lights as large as tractor tires to expose the actors
in a favorable glow. Colonial homes are stout with kids

testing younger hunger inside Chevys and Plymouths
and Fords. By midnight the stage has become Bethlehem
Steel, and tired hands of the gaggle of workers switch

off electricity and lounge with drowsy reprieve
for days to come slinging 2 by 4s to reinvent the world.

TAKING COVER

I watch finches streak beyond
the glass, imagine life
without shame
without having done it all at a tilt.

Tomorrow rain might come
for good, the earth's strained
crops desperate and licking their lips
under abused terrain.

Hemispheres of the brain
are inundated with this life
contained in them

as if the mind is
a cupboard, a cavernous place
my mother would scavenge
for relief of forgotten
wine, for smells of dried lilac

and cooking sherry
disappearing more
quickly than the meals
she poured the spirit into as

she stirred and stirred
with her hands fluttering
like parakeets above

the stew as it bubbled over—
killing the flame
until my father got home, his

dread on fire as he found his wife
so changed from the love

he had left in the morning. Home
in the afternoon I mastered duties
to hide liquor, set a table, put cutting
boards on the counter, yank

apart celery stalks
with my hand on her hand
to take the knife away before

my father's cautious head
nudged through the door
and like a match to gasoline
the words of blame invaded

the house and left
my ears shuttered against bellows
of the fight. With a flurry
of feet I let the screen door tremble
behind me where empty, sinuous

roads ran like rapids beneath
my flight and the boys
swooped in to make me

weightless beneath stabs of a sizzling
sun, its heat inked into us
our sneakers running
and running into the vistas
from only so much we could take.

WHISPERS AND VOWS

The mothers were the ones who explained secrets
like *no one tells you how it's going to be*

—meaning, *when you get old.*

On a walk on my street last week a young man
reached his hand to touch my arm as I turned

my ankle with a shock to the bones twisted
flush against the ground, balance collapsed

as if a 4-inch heel had snapped from its very sole.

A year ago it seems we would have laughed
the awkwardness off and his eyes would be bold,
would easily find mine, and like

a blood rotation around the body we'd give in
to attraction that would take us
to a bed and a simple breeze would show itself

and slant across the room to cool us off
as we rolled away from the other body, sidelong

glances to our nakedness and the sweat
on his skin would lift me from him, then I would

dress and leave. My ache today is masculine, tough

along the fringe like my father was, resistant
and toying with age until he was too old to deny it.

I miss a person's touch and gentle gestures
that show what I am made of. Another mother's

lesson is how growing the years breeds
change *whether we want it or not* and I take

a vow to know composure, benevolence, to open
clenched fists and cause no one any more harm.

ELEGY ONE: LETTING GO

> *Most*
> *of my decisions have been wrong*
> —Larry Levis

As my father lay dying
I said in a voice lower than I use with the living,
you were right about everything. He was quick
to reply that I said it only because
he was dying, to make him feel good, and with a huff
through my breath canal, I swore I would not
appease him at this stage in a mismanaged world
when all that mattered was truth. He smiled as far as dying
allowed him, the day typical Southern California non
descript and sunny and dry, unusual clouds somehow wrong
in the sky. He reached over the rail of his bed to grab me
as he would with his "whip of always being right" and without
ability to swallow, said nothing. I looked at him
like a child in a rush of need, collapsing, as he was
beneath the weight of too many of my wrong decisions.
I stroked his hand marked by spots of age, stopping my gaze
on the lightest hair he wore above his wrists like a sleeve, eyes
sunken into sockets that appeared too large. He slept
without dying for a while, without that wag of caution
in his finger, without that glare of criticism that could spread
like a badlands in front of me. And without acerbic words
for mistakes I had made, I imagined he was trying to say
he could forgive me for all the things I had done
so wrong, and as the last hour of the day shook off
certainty of the sun, I could hear him mumble
that perhaps it was the two of us
who were right about everything.

GREAT ESCAPES

After the first martini she is radiant, persevering man beside her delighted by a flourish of her hand as he goes on with his story of a dog run down in Beverly Hills, and he does go on, tidbits regarding the market, wizardry of masseurs, and soon the drone of him makes her love the ease of ordering another, mind skipping lightly to the edge of a fuzzy universe where she uncorks at the waist as he slips his hand between her hip and the bar stool she steps from like she's coming off a train. Sailing to the john, her black pump shoves the door open to green-tiled basin, its surface slick and gleaming like a mirror, and by morning a note says he carried her, she was light as air, and he leaves her two aspirin, a lost earring, his out-of-town number. When she wakes I make her breakfast of tomato juice with vodka, study how pepper twirls but never mixes in, a sadness settled in her like a tiny hotel where the pain resides, where she wanders its halls and checks in on traveling lovers, on the dead, on our father screaming at us for something no one did. When I leave she clicks the chaise down, one, two, three, reminds me to bury her in our hometown, in Renton, reminds me to dance on her grave the way we did when they buried Jimi Hendrix under a plaque no larger than an oversized Hershey bar, his grandmother next to him under identical plaque, dead at one hundred, sleeping with one eye open just a stride away, a stride away, simple vigilant stride away.

PETTABLE WALLPAPER

The day is muddy in my mouth, a fight breaks out next door, and I imagine Annie in the roomy tub, bubbles up to her neck, knees jutted through gentle water, pencil stuck through her raisin-black hair. I reach for the bathroom door, its threshold seeming to be off its hinges, no suds, no flesh peeking into the air, porcelain sink studded with sullied-red wads of cotton, a flitter of the smell of Witch Hazel, threads of blood dusted on white linoleum floor glossy as a china plate. I bump into Annie like she is a sack of dying fruit, mirror cracked, her body fallen against the wall covered by furry flowered wallpaper, arm lost above her like she needs to keep the ceiling off the floor. I can almost feel the drug pulsing through her, touching every organ, and I pull my sister to me, the weight of her like a statue dragged from its base, cradle her until the siren closes in, until I know they have come for us, and it does come, ambulance clipping the lawn for neighbors to see, rush of men to the floor with medical gear flying out of bags like birds from a cage. The red truck rockets through town with the man who doesn't drive side by side with Annie as my heart disconnects from her terrible choices and I hold my breath, hold her limp hand that pushed in the drug, paramedics adjusting IV and oxygen like she is a bomb to be defused, as if the looming act of pumping her empty could return a failing system to its normal living function, and the air that flushes inside me now is more smother than relief, every nerve waiting for the next time, for this time to be undone.

ELEGY TWO: KNOWING

My mother is dying and I am the only one
who knows it. On days she is at peace
she brushes her hair fifty times and looks like
Ava Gardner, manages my eggs, my favorite
shirt, the timing of the bus. Days like that
she and I *own it*, roll it around in our hands
and then I imagine it's years later, people
cooing how much I look like her, how
pensive I've become with omnivorous eyes
of a pelican. On days she starts drinking
misery sits with me at school and when
the bus dumps me home at four she
is weaving, smoking, a hole in her dress,
asleep on her side collapsed into shame,
and suddenly I am running with impatient
boys, staring at a kid's chest measuring how
tall he is—the same time watching the house
where mother breathes like an anvil weighs
down her torso in almost invisible tremors
so I drive her to a shop for liquor without
any smell until one afternoon she slips away.
The last time I run into her is in a dream
years after her death on a downtown street
where I live, her wavy hair lifted like a kite
and we talk with a strain that snaps muscle
from bone, questions like where have I been?
did I go to college? how's my father? and I
answer carefully as I did when she drank. She
asks what I do and I say *film* and her head tilts

in a gesture of interest, says she wants to see
one I made, and I tell her *yes*, don't want to be
pushy, her stance shying away as I suggest
she call me when she's got the time. Traffic
moves like a parade as she turns without
the touch she used to rub on me with a salve,
our separation like a dance and I step back
from her sudden transparency lost in a crowd
and when I wake at home in my clothes flat
against my body, I see she is not my mother
now and I am not among the dead with secrets
held tightly inside her of why she had to leave.

SECTION THREE

THE DAVIDS

I didn't know how to be around people
in the drawn out years of thirst and grief

so I followed volatile currents, learned to tack

across a river without turning on the juice,
belief in the rudder, reliance on the wind.

Those days the house was disheveled

and in a fog my lover and I slept
as the garbage truck cleared our alley. We were

desperate to believe a toss of remnants

is a lucky sign like flights of birds who aim
toward the window and in quickened

moments veer from their reflections, simple lessons

of being lost and coming back again. I am ragged
from dodging fleets of arrows, asking why

I disappointed the kind ones—like the opulence

of Davids—uncle, cousins, high school drummer,
teachers, true love, boyfriends and a cook.

Why one strays into a band of wandering men
to lie awake with too many hands on so many

bodies is not really a mystery, but it becomes wise

to give up the flock for the one. Yet mine demanded
convention: *say this, buy that, forget him,* sex

in a bed, promise to return, and when he drove

away he disappeared. Again, a hurtle
of men without the measure of breath to keep me

above water. Soon absence and inertia

lapsed into unexplained peace, my indistinct eyes
cast inward with a pleasant release to fly solo,

to fill a sail with wind at my back, surprise

of another David with unexpected footfall
arriving after extravagant miles through the dark.

PRESCRIPTIVE FICTION
FOR INSOMNIA

To Tobias Wolff

I read Wolff in the middle of the night
as though he's woken me

                     and whispers
*why don't you pick me up, chew on a story
or two* and I grin madly, tumble pillows

into a balanced stack to prop me up,
legs stretched like a cat's,
                     the mind picking
synopses to lure me in devious directions.

He's not the only writer who makes me
think how uncomplicated I am,
                     such little reference

to Faulkner, Pynchon, the Russians
and Proust. I never really know
                     if I lust for the writer
                     or for the pen,

for the words I tussle with, my lips
                     moving to wild
syntax and rhythms that spin me

round, round—like a record, baby,
besotted with language and how
mighty our transcendence is.

Last night, I dropped J.D. to my stomach
after I'd put down Tobias and a wild-eyed
Japanese writer demanding
                        too much work
                        at 2 a.m. when

my voices sing to me, *you're no good*
                        you're no good,
                        you're no good

until early into dawn when I surrender
to slumber and sink beneath comforters

with Wolff's last-ditch story
of a guy shot in a pool hall whose time
in this world is brief, breathless,

a high-speed bank-shot of final thoughts
leaping across a single page
                        as a bullet furrows
                        into his brain.

In this mob of climax and verdict
I marvel at the souls so unlike me

and I drift off to sleep with the channelers
who fork over all the human
                        nitty-gritty there is.

A DAY OFF

A drip is distant and persistent
like steady intravenous, buckwheat
noodles stuck to a Calphylon pot
soaking in the sink. Should I leave that
wedding gift to dress itself in rust?
Will it survive the scourge of alchemy
longer than the marriage did? His claim
we made an error in judgment—
euphemism for *mistake*—sits like a sign
clanging in the wind. I stay in
underwear and my last lover's shirt
and order meat from the pick-up
place as I hurtle through ways this day
will stagger into glorious sloth, effort
beyond one foot as the other is laid
to rest, escape from drive-by murder
with Penn and Duvall dressed in shotguns,
double-breasted armor from Armani.
Three weeks of plain clothes go down
the laundry chute as I clasp a helmet
under my chin, clip a bulb to the front
to see how far I can go into plunge
and disappearance. The actors
as cops are renegade and the phony
gangsters fight a war they cannot win
in blue and red colors and no one
is what they say they are in the movies.
The phone rings and I let it go, unable
to answer to anyone, and even on a day

off I hear sounds of guns, the street
clogged by a pounding from metal spikes
that gouge a hole large enough to slip
a person through where it's iffy to be
found. I throw on a jacket, give a tender
tap to my helmet in the cold night as I
lean across the hole to stare into the void
and decide to send the canaries down first.

BLEED

The blood moves through the body in a circle, moving into the heart and then back out of it on the other side.

The List reminds me what to do, who to co-mingle with, and every day I add a different task, plan meals, shell out a bundle for excess and self-pleasure. Before noon I make it to the grocery, the warehouse where UPS takes things back, garden shop showing off succulents in the wrong season for peonies, dog trainer for Maxie's bites and yowls, a thousand dollars to the bank to pump up possibility I will be all right. My husband is not on my list any longer, circling through me without returning to the heart, sudden failings swept to the side of the house where the dog snarls and flares his mouth. My hours for sleep in tossing-churning nights have faded with the stars and leave me weary as I stand at the window and see how rain has frozen and slabbed the mountains with snow. Purity and glisten bleed from the clouds strung along the sky circling peaks above the valley, acres of shadow like an overflow of woefulness in this town where the real comes in one side and surreal flows out the other. The city suffers from *worst* bloated traffic, *best* deceptive hustle, and he wants my bare, shivering flesh, its chafing and reshaping of us as he drags his hands along my difficult bones. I have pleased too many people and scampered too hard, and still I believe survival and justice are within reach. The morning bleeds into a sharp-edged day and I kick aside flung clothes to clear a path to the end of dishevelment and phone him to say this isn't enough, this re-routing of our life, our fist-sized hearts losing rhythm. I know I will bleed a surfeit of tears and the dog licking my face will save me from regret. I open the drapes onto the oddity of snow in a place eternally doused in sunlight, its soundless devotion reliable in the way blood fills the wings of a bird before it takes off in enviable flight.

FLIGHT #505

The day I thought I was going to die
on a commercial flight in a chaotic display
of thunderclouds and nearness to the hidden sun
                                  a calm of feeling

good about where I was in life—with much less
trauma, some unusual bliss of work—closed in

around me. There was the odd charm of certitude
and a cloak of dying-doing-what-one-loves
that warmed me like a satin-lined camel-haired
coat I wear in New York.

        Distance from LAX to JFK made me—
and the whole mass of people strapped in and facing
only one direction toward the pilots—hope

that experience in the cockpit was precise
in its busyness of handling emergency.

                There was imminence of disaster

that prodded the mind to begin a dialogue with weather
and gravity. Scanning every horizon, air traffic
controllers spoke mouthfuls of code from their towers,

analyzing data from screens for high-altitude platoons
of jets to land where the lightning allowed,
in the same way a father might gauge obstacles
with his kids in the car in the snow. In times like this

                it seems wise for the pilots' cabin doors

to remain locked. People on the plane changed
from readers, sleepers, snackers to creatures making
panicked sounds and clinging to someone next
to them—full of sudden

                mumbling, fretting, expecting
                the messiness of death

as if plummet was a given condition of the deal
of flying high above the earth in a carefully
concocted mass of metal that hoists people as far

away as we can go. But the storms were shifting, showing
off, three at once, a gaggle above the Atlantic coast
like a military threat or losing oneself in a gorge

                of flooded streams. Beside me

was the gift of a sturdy, sexy man climbing
toward my age, without realistic concern, with
briefcase and a blue tie. No holiday event or funeral
service or baby being born had forced me

to fly to the house I'd grown up in, but I was beholden
to research and a journey to lost childhood
friends. In other words, I was almost home.

       Weather piled into greater threats and chats
with Mr. Handsome in a business suit dissolved
into a fear people wisely have when 30,000
feet above the earth, as sky-high clouds bullied us

from New York to Philly to Jersey to Baltimore to DC,
jet fuel dissipating, wings unprepared for ice

and bending toward break. Winds assaulted
the body of the plane shifting storable baggage
in its bins, sounding like war shot straight to the heart.

The beautiful man was a talker but silence
bathed us both as no one came to comfort us—
attendants unable to balance in upright positions—

          and in this state of shock his hand

fell onto my thigh, his fingers crawling from his lap
to my hair, to the rigid skin of my ear. Without
a thought to stand on, we flew into desperate

kissing as if our lips would feel their last, as if
going down to the ground together would be
the best route to heaven. Fearless in our lewd behavior

            we could have missed the sudden glory

of controlled descent at survivable speed

       as we whipped our heads toward the oval
window, eyes seeking the ground, pilots' voices
like the whisper of a hundred words of love.

I knew I would never see the dark-haired man again
as we changed imaginary eulogies
to swallowed farewells in a corral

of twenty jets on bulging tires waiting for cargos
of fuel as our heads fell back, feet heavy
and numb, the rain wilted to drizzle and seeping in

       to the anchored unfazed beloved
       caress-able steadfast tarmac.

CAR WARS

1.
First the crash, then raining glass and heavy metal in the flying dust on Riverside Drive. Two men the size of two men rise up from half-cocked doors, cacophony of overlapping words like, *idiot, moron, asshole, reckless-sonofabitch-you.*

2.
Blam blam blam say the weapons dressed up as cars, bumpers thumped chest to chest the way players celebrate a winning goal. Traffic deaths rise this year in a spate of collisions that speed outside our windows in front of our eyes within inches of reach. The men look off into sun-blitzed hills and think how this life could be overhauled.

3.
On the hill I observe the men flanking mangled cars, their understandable dread of police charging to the scene. Fury, and blame blame, blame are amplified as ornamented car hoods sing *darlin' you oo oo oo send me* into the front of that nice BMW, the Porsche and its detonated airbag slumped, draining another sports car of seduction and speed.

4.
In my chaise lounge I lie at a distance, parked for the day with nowhere to go, no one to swoon me, flurry of lizards slipping underneath the wildflowers and grass. Above it all, I see the roadside crew bend to survey the damage. Soon a pair of tow trucks will arrive. Information will be tested and everyone is soaked in solitude.

5.
Unmuffled threats rev up again until I hear the cop yell *stop*, one arm out and the palm of his hand up like a Supreme singing *In the Name of Love*. Voices in my ear buds speak of common citizens going to the moon someday soon, escaping the gnarled tangles of civilization.

6.
My friend sends a telephone ring that sounds like a pianist in my pocket. She and I sport mental tattoos of racing down boulevards in cars with boys smoking weed, their fingertips thumbing a vinyl dash in time to *Baby You Can Drive My Car*. I tell her how accidents in vehicles, even deadly, drive us to the brink of voyeurism, how drivers call automobiles *Her* in lieu of real women.

7.
The hill above the wreck is littered with headlight shards, coyote tracks, empty bottles of beer. Far beneath me the men surrender information the way the government likes it. Traffic creeps and sluggish cruisers steer clear of one another as drivers brake to avoid kissing the car in front of them, fingers pointed to the side of the road, mumbling, *There. There but for the grace of God . . .*

SWIMMING WITH HOMELESS MEN WHO SLEEP BENEATH THE PIER

A few men scheme along the surfer beach
with long-handled discs in silent hover

above the sand, their white hair tailing
the sweep of their machines as they discover

metal like nickels and quarters, burnished, slinky
bracelets and Bolo ties. Another cadre of men sleep

under the pier in late afternoon, merciful
siesta to a lull of the waves and when they wake

I drag out of the water, tie my hair back, sit
in dampness beside the line of them staring across

the sea. Their brown-skinned bodies wear stories
of battles that had raged in Filipino jungles or inside

hideouts of Saigon, this Pacific shore similar
to the kindness they can slip their minds around

without a war. My friend Joseph tended to the men
until he became one of them, my instinct still to seek

him out as I stroll along the soft grainy earth
where it is driven into a line of cliffs dropped toward

low-tide coves, a man and his shadow loping by
the endless blue water until he rests during his trek

to Pt. Mugu talking to seagulls before he saunters on.
Delia was Joe's enchantress and when he lost

her he believed in alien beings for a while, married
a wild girl who became famous as if craziness

were an art, and now the evening tides wash in
and the men untangle fishing lines as if nylon threads

are lives they meant to lead, and my hair comes undone
the way Joe liked it, handfuls scrambled by the breeze.

CALLING IN GONE

Sometimes I brew a cup of tea or grind an odorous orange to its rind and imagine I have a farm, remember my son, reluctant student blowing through the door with a life-size cup of Java and his new-professor blues. Where I begin the day is unseen like a deer nibbling a leaf. My garden shows off gardenia buds, sweet peas and squash begins to lengthen into itself. A Mexican tin-framed mirror over the sink tells me a thing or two how age is having its way with me, teaches the art of reflection and flipping the bird. Magical potions plump my flesh with cryptic chemical agents that give no explanation of how they intend to remake my face. I want to love my labor, love my neighbor, *love love love*, as the Beat Boys said, and yet I am stuck on *pause* with nothing but digital drudge to tell me what to do. Muscles glide over bones like snakes, history hibernates inside me as I work more than I do anything else. In the threshold of the door, a panoply of air touches my hair, my skin in its robe, and someday I will call in sick and tired, release myself from other people's needs, sprout courage for better-laid plans to bloom like aftermath of a birth from its seed.

ROUGH TRADE

There is a poster of an ape on the wall, mouth wide,
holding a rock above his head twice the size of his hand

and in his other grip he mangles a strip of film
that flutters like a tattered flag. The movie is nailed

into place by numbers on a hard drive, the room

open past its bedtime. The man who keeps me late
has grey tincture to his face and likes to call out *honey*

babysweetheart, as he touches my weary shoulder
to signal he wants me to *cut*   the shot   *here*.

The machine heats to a hum and my fingers almost

blister on the knob in constant shuttle from stop to go.
Illusion subdues reason. I slide a fancy netted-seat chair

back from the screen and his mood is brooding, perhaps
unhappy with me, with my choices, and buttons

of his shirt have come undone. With him I keep the number
of studio security in my pocket, and critical to survival

and keeping my job, I lie to him, convince him my son

is coming home, that I must unlock the door to meet
and feed the kid a late-night meal. The man never

ever knows I don't have a son or if I did he wouldn't care
as I exit the place through a land of innuendo and close in

the ape, the boss who doesn't look up, dangerous smoke
filling the room the way special effects create disaster. He

lights a cigarette in the dark, takes a hit and I leave him
perhaps forever, as he sits by himself in his radioactive glow.

ONLY SO MUCH

There is scattershot emphasis from me the mother and Dave the boyfriend. I never see his lips frozen in the last syllable he spoke the way I do today. My son is a prodigy of escape and blows through two rooms as he runs off and I miss him quickly like sky changing from blue to rain. My words dart around my mouth like hummingbird wings in a flurry of accusation. I become quiet and see he has turned away. *There, I said it*, I say, which I don't actually say out loud but to myself as if owning the last words will change everything. He starts in on me, does not re-decide, does not restrain threats, careless of how dialogue can be a thing like a brick. My son guns the car outside and I look at Dave and we take on each other's gestures: hand smacking the forehead, strike of the foot on the ground at what has fallen and won't get picked up, language stuck on *have to-need to-you don't understand* bunched together in a dying bouquet. I forget where we started and sink my hands into dishwater. I see how the morning has become a scrim across Dave's eyes and soon he will see something else as he walks to a separate part of the house where he and the dog will tussle and pant away demons. The water is a blur of poached eggs as I free it down the drain, and it disappears like sounds only the dog can hear of birds resettling on the fence, the sighs of humans whimpering and coming undone.

SECTION FOUR

THE RETRIEVAL: AIRPORT: DAY

Before my wait for Sander ends in a eureka of sorts, before we kiss and mumble things like, *ah, here you are* and *mmm, I missed you*, I run into a celebrity I worked for and he remembers me but is *in a terrible hurry* and dismisses me like a pet. It seems wise to go outside with the smokers to get away from any feeling I should soothe his discomfort because he was my boss, but fear of what Sander's kids call Cancer Sticks urges on a picture of being unable to tread forward for more than a block. A voice erupts from the ceiling changing Sander's arrival time as if it's a creative decision, inciting a change in my direction—quick U-turn to exit the low-slung building painted with a murkiness from smog like there's a plague over the city.

A two-van accident gets sorted, passengers push, shove for immediate police attention that might allow them to make their planes. My hand moves to the side of my body that houses the liver where a trio of ribs are sore enough to hinder movement and I wonder what Sander will imagine when I tell him I missed a couple steps on our staircase. Perhaps he can't imagine scenarios of abuse, his world ordered and predictable, but it *was* the stairs, and of course I tell Sander when we meet that I tumbled, and of course he believes me.

After *I missed you*, and, *yeah, missed you too*, after he avoids the bruised area to rub the small of my back, Sander loads me up with details of the trip and I take in smells of the restaurants lined up like row houses. Perhaps I don't listen well as he says something I don't take in the first time and asks again, *When's your next job start?* We have grown apart, and I look at him as if he's asked for an algebraic equation. He no longer asks the right questions, like how do we do something else, and for the first time since we started, his homecoming is especially morose as the automatic doors swing open to let one of us break out of the terminal first.

HISTORY REPEATS ITSELF, REPEATS ITSELF

> *The whole world is watching . . .*
> Demonstrators' chant—Democratic Convention—1968

1.
On the porch Maggie's daughter, the size of a Great Dane, in thrift-store snowsuit scrapes one leg past the other, opens the flaps of a television-sized carton, hands cold despite mittens attached by safety pins to each sleeve. The box is the size of her world, her mother inside pawing through mail and sales ads for offers she can't afford. Husband or dad, depending on who remembers him, is supposed to be alive in Iraq, Maggie and the girl finding solace in freezing weather with bone soup on a single-burner stove, in clothes Maggie makes from other clothes.

2.
Fire burns up the chimney, its ashes causing the soldier's wife to wheeze from scorched kindling of front-page news that repeats itself, repeats itself—the president a criminal and still no jail, no death by shame, not one rusty nail to seal his coffin.

3.
People surge into the streets, the too-young-to-fail saving trees, bodies close as nerve endings striking pavement of the boulevard to stop the Nazis, stop the guns, stop the chemicals flown onto food, stop the murder of black women's children killed by police. And killed by police. In history, mothers rage against wars and how it takes their sons; and then the next ones.

4.
The young girl paws the inside of the box tipped over onto the porch. The house reshapes itself under eaves burdened with snow as Maggie rubs her hands, pulls her shoulders around her chest to create warmth, uncrates the girl, swoops her inside, kicks the door to close against the cold. Dinner is flimsy but there is wood, short pile of children's books, black and white tv, the girl sitting on the floor between her mother's legs, her hands around Maggie's tapered calves like prisoners' hands around the bars.

5.
On the news protesters stand face to face with police, messages scrawled on torn sides of cardboard boxes, fingers in fists, fingers spread in peace signs, police staring down another mother of a dead son, and just like parents who stand in the street waiting for their kids to hustle home after one of the weapons sends another child to unsuspecting death—here we go—here we go again.

1968

The highway ambles north, a lesson in perspective as we sway to a trio of guitar chords that make the players mythical, bass line cutting like a dagger through cigarettes and pot, erratic breathing. We stop for food, call a friend from the tall glass booth leaning on the side of the road who tells us the coastal college is crawling with rebellion, classes empty of students spending first semester in the streets, police landing nightsticks that open flesh and no one fast enough to get away from tear gas. The boy in our car sleeps, *like the dead* the driver says, aiming us straight to the Canadian border on the boy's birthday, his unlucky number sending him to the draft, to Vietnam, secretly to Cambodia and Laos. The afternoon gets muggy and drowsiness makes us roll down windows, shaggy hair streaked by the wind when the music stops, as if the road has ended, someone's voice throaty and solemn to interrupt the numbing hum of tires, to announce that Martin Luther King has been shot. The car drifts to the side of the road. The boys in the backseat rush into sudden clutch like trying to stop human plummet from a cliff. Perhaps the man yammers on. Perhaps the car is tilted, the engine shutting down. We are swabbed in silence, nothing to discuss, to consider, to envision, except the certainty we could have stopped that bullet, caught that 30-aught-6 rifle round and snuffed it with our bared teeth.

ALONE IN THE STORM

Darkness rumbles like stillness after a murder and before police arrive on the scene and everything is crisis. Jack drives off as if he wants to chase the storm, trusting me to handle indelicate weather, perhaps lightning. I wait for him to return with sandbags and rubber boots he mistakenly calls booties the way he does when I wag my butt and lure him to me. Every strand of hair tangles with the wind and I want to call my son because lately he seems to know everything, is addicted to the art of rescue, but distraction is compounded by swells of the tempest and its greed. I grit my teeth as patio chairs begin to shimmy from their glue and the sky sends its deluge of rain. Topsoil spins into a devil of debris, its cone gobbling a story I wrote under the moon before days of easy living turned nasty, tempers cooking in confusion. A sudden cyclone shows no discretion as it steals my watering can and pricey jeweled watch Jack cinched around my wrist to remember when to love him, a gift perhaps for us both as he and I move from drought to flood as easily as I buy excess food when the family gathers for holidays the way bees smother a hive and light strafes the hills. Juggernauts of motion toss pots of begonias like paper lanterns, the storm taking knickknacks off tables like bones flung from a plate. The men in my life bluster through disaster as I wait for them to call and ask if I'm all right beneath gray animal clouds dumping more water, and no one to answer my questions of why Jack drove off without his raincoat, why instinct doesn't chuck me back into the house, what day the storm will stop kicking up sand that blows miles and miles from the ocean and throw in its goddamn towel.

CAUTIONARY TALE

It is habit to send the canary in first, to watch it flit into corners of the kitchen where my husband and I roost on respective sides of the room, stack avocado, basil and cheese on toast despite our lack of hunger. I watch the bird test distance as it heads into the bedroom to investigate our imprint under the quilt. Finding our souls had not detached from our bodies during the night, the bird sings to announce this victory, lifting off with its dedication to unearth danger, flying along the ceiling to the patio where my husband and I read wild tales of how our species treat one another, so in love we were for a while, so certain and careful. Outside, I fear the bird will flee, yellow wings stretched and thinking it is someone else. I order it to double-back inside to check pockets of blue jeans where it finds another woman's number curved against double stitching, then on to check my husband's mouth where every sentence lately is fabrication. The bird seems a bit too charmed by its discoveries and I imagine it works for my husband when I am gone, today's mission lapsing into a false sense of completion as it settles on my shoulder to peck beneath feathers layered with such complexity I feel nothing but envy for the stratified weave that insulates it in terrible weather.

LYING ON THE FLOOR AND LYING TO ONESELF ARE EQUAL IN STATURE

> *Age is something that doesn't matter, unless you are a cheese.*
>
> —Luis Buñuel

One day with birds at the window and pastries in the oven, a smear of grease grabs my rubber sole and pitches me into the sink and like a ball off a 9-iron the lean clink of head onto blemished linoleum forces my eyesight to sail into the distance. If I were a person with deliberation and calm I might have learned to gaze at the steps I take, to recover quickly before I am prone on my own floor. I feel the cool of the surface like a child post-tantrum and ask if there are better ways to avoid the rabbit hole. Oh, fuck it, I think, let me take a minute to recover from shame of instability and the ability to save myself, some slip of breeze flitting through the window to soothe me. The body knows there is nowhere to go but up, so I push with a working woman's hands, a twist of torso, a heft in my knees to stand at five foot one and pat myself down finding the bones have held themselves together.

My day goes on, and I make fifty more mistakes, achieve a few good deeds like pitching mail into recycle bins that teach us to use things more than once. My friend phones, says we should cruise the bars like days of sex without love and I tell her *yes*, time for a prison break and wishful thinking we are young in some low-lit club, the cloth of a man's shirt brushing my back as he reaches for another drink and turns too close to my face to ask if I want one, and I will say *yes*. I will dress in ambiguous clothes before my friend swings by and we will flirt, sip double-barreled specialty drinks, eat from a platter of diverse cheeses, accidentally bump a couple guys' thighs and lose a little balance against their table. We will remember the years they would ask us home, certain we will never hear those words again as we get into our valeted car with a little heat in the seats, observing the signs and weaving back into ourselves at the big bang of midnight.

COME ON AND TAKE IT

> *. . . each time I tell myself I think I've had enough,*
> *I'm gonna show you, baby, that a woman can be tough*
> —Janis Joplin

I always knew something was wrong with the movie business. Making movies is synonymous with being Someone, with knowing privilege and being protected from mundane dramas of real life. In this company town I can't stop seeing scenes from the business played back to me. To this day, I still throw myself into the clutch of the wrong men, drink too much, and nerves in my body fall asleep. As I slink about in corners of strip-searching situations, or I can't find my scarf and purse and keys, I still wait to be saved in the last ten minutes of the final reel. Bosses loved to flaunt language like *courage, academy award performance, astonishing moment, great legs, come to poppa*, and just like that my mind roams like a flurry on a slide guitar. In movies characters somehow manage shock and fear in situations we could never actually handle when a hooded person with a 10-inch knife stands over our beds while we sleep. Sometimes there is the bluster of an actress strutting into a room on the edge of a plunging hill where she flops on a sofa, kicks off red-soled Louboutin heels, shows dismay without wrinkling skin or hair and curses the latest man, saying dialogue like, *I shoulda' killed the bastard*. A producer used to tap my shoulder and tell me he wanted to linger on the actresses' pouty lips so that every woman in the audience wanted to be her. I'd spin the knob to leap further into the scripted plot of another bank job, and the she-thief might seduce the top-dog robber who appeared from somewhere unknown, perhaps from the balcony through an unlocked door. A weariness would come over me, and I wanted to weep from small inconsequential things like running out of cat food. Like a lightning strike, he would yell at me to *toughen up*, I'm *too nice*, and on weekends I believed him, avoided people who took gentle meanderings along the ocean and learned how to jump out of airplanes instead. It could be hard on the spine and shoulders but I was young and believed everything would heal. The producer could mangle the air with a throat clearing and without closure, might say, *I gotta meet a guy who knows a guy*, so *wrap it up*, and I'd hear choral music as if I were about to be sprung from the slammer. My stomach chattered for food as I shut the machine down when suddenly, with sweetness, he called his daughter, which like too many unremarkable things almost made me cry. He told her he knows a guy and she can have what they both want at the coveted college across town, as in no test scores, and a starting position on the soccer team. There was pause for her voice, then producer laughed and answered, *piece of cake*, and I got hungrier, which made me forget if this was a movie or some version of real life, and whether I should stay in a wide shot or go into a close-up as she said, *thank you, daddy, I love you, daddy.* Everybody does.

LOVE FALLEN TO THE GROUND

1.
It does zoom by when I think about it. Life, I mean. Birds in a storm. Whoosh, *hello, goodbye.* Everyone so afraid. Of death, I mean, of 200 species a day dying without a gravestone, clear-cut homes flattened to ash in blazes worse than . . . Worse than what? When memory spits like bees, I remember my small legs bent in a hunch over fur-topped holes in the yard where bunnies huddled. Before I'd reach inside, or as I did, my mother would say, *don't touch the babies or their mothers will leave them.* Another nature story. Often, we slink away from touch, but most days she corralled me with her hand cupped around my elbow to lead me on this path, or another, out of the disappearing woods to find gentlest ways to grow me. When we tell a story, we often start with, *feels like yesterday . . .* then action and consequence, understandable doubt.

2.
Does memory flash like life before our eyes as they say it does? The flammable hills in a drought, limping creatures in dying grass, light, light, damn light along his back in flapping shirt through the field of vines, death of horses on a racetrack buckling to the dirt, my husband weaving on a ship deck before we leave the port, his breath snaked around my hair, the snake on our picnic rock, kissing in stairwells, kissing in public before we reached the top floor.

3.
The body itches to shed itself and my vision wafts through the room where our years together chafe like wind chimes. This town is getting swept back to its second layer, sometimes by fire, sometimes by the days we knew so much—abundant food dropped from trees, protection of mountain tops cleaned like feathers from fowl, disappearance of animals taken for granted the way a lizard loses a tail, jungles lose cover to machetes. The night brings on smell of gasoline, smack of a car door, voice insistent with *hello, hello, anybody there?* I walk out into the sigh of exodus taking over the city, warm air against the skin, soft scents mumbling through windows, a hand fallen across my face so that finally I can sleep.

THE FUTURE

To David Parry

When Gabriel and I went flying, he disregarded flight rules and when I'd worry about getting busted for his illegal ways, he'd say, *What are they going to do, shoot us down?* Without warning he would drop the plane to outlawed altitude, flip us upside down over the San Fernando Valley then roll us back over in a beeline to the ocean.

On a walk on the beach one day my husband says to me, years ahead of dying, that he wants to be buried in a sunny plot at the popular hillside cemetery and I say *buried* as if it's a taste of rotten fish, and he says he wants to stay intact, to slowly be trifled into dust. I tell him to set me on fire, my body combusted into ash, my final wish to be scattered from a plane. He stares as if I have already vanished, tells me he wouldn't know what to do. I hook my arm through the crook of his as we stroll like brand new lovers and I tell him to drive to Santa Monica Airport, find Gabriel and let him know you're there to take me where he knows I want to go.

Gabriel will ask all about us as he straps you in, and he will climb right out of the city where you'll feel as far as you can get from trouble and grief. You'll watch the earth fall away, split into land on one side and sea on the other, and you will climb and climb until he tells you it's time, and you will open the window to jimmy my container of ashes out of the small glass square, shaking me out in a dark transparent flow as I travel into the folds of deep blue sky.

I will seem heavier than anything you've ever handled as Gabriel strums a knob in the cockpit and asks, *Is she gone yet*, and to the rhythm of the engine you'll nod your head no, and I can already hear him say, *Well, keep pouring her out, I can't stay up here forever.*

CLIMBING OUT OF QUARANTINE ONE LIMB AT A TIME

Neighbors emerge beneath thresholds to meet without touch in the street, their arms picking up the city news and bits of flung cups dropped by walkers with their dogs. We are still protected by masks and distance from opposite curbs. I seem to be returning to the *she* of my life again, familiar face in the mirror and necessary chores have a clearer path through obstacle courses of clutter in the rooms. The work of sorting out other people's lives curves my shoulders over the desk and though they say we will return to office buildings soon, the shut-in light is still bad so I pull up blinds that separate me from acrobatic squirrels in the trees. I soothe myself by taking the car into hills that surround the city, my mind in a fury of mutterings about mundane matters, and memory is a companion that makes me remember only what I have forgotten. I ascend a trail that smells of dirt and evergreen, and suck breath through my mask under a blue sky that strides along the ridge of the mountains. A family trudges toward me, walking down from exhilaration and release. They move to the side of the trail and I move to mine, the kids with flushed faces. The parents nod. The boy says something about snakes, in a muffle behind his child's mask and the woman shakes her head no with what may, underneath, be a grin. The family passes me toward protection of their own home. The wind picks up as I descend in a slight jog to where the car sits alone. The drive home is short and something within my control. I slink into the garage where it is dark, illuminated by those crazy headlights that glow before a switch turns them on—for safety, the salesman said—and almost like invocation, there is a glint from my lost bracelet near the rakes and shovels and firewood, an exiled dazzle in the murk of what has changed us.

ACKNOWLEDGEMENTS

Angle of Reflection (Anthology)—"Don't Wait Up" (originally published as "Working the Weekend")

Askew—"Great Escapes"

Beyond the Lyric Moment: An Anthology Inspired by Southern California Workshops with David St. John, edited by Jim Natal, Cathie Sandstrom and Lynne Thompson—"Whispers and Vows" (originally published as "Driving Home from the Gym")

Beyond Words (April 2021 issue)—"Invisible"

Blue Mountain Review—"Inner Ear"

Psychological Perspectives—"Her" (originally published as "When the Children Are Gone"), "Day One" and "Rough Trade"

San Diego Poetry Annual—"Swimming with Homeless Men Who Live Beneath the Pier"

Sheila-Na-Gig—"Knowing" and "Under the Influence"

Spillway # 27—"Letting Go"

Spillway #28—"Lying On the Floor and Lying to Oneself Are Equal in Stature"

Spillway #29—"Don't Get Up" and "that lingering need for ritual"

NOTES

Epigraph
Elizabeth Hardwick, "In the Wasteland"
New York Review of Books, 1996

Page 23
Olivier Messiaen and Arnold Schoenberg were European classical music composers who became known for atonal music and what is often now called "new music" or simply, 20th century music.

Page 29
Jimi Hendrix is buried in Renton, Washington. He and his grandmother are buried side by side under small rectangular plaques with their names and the dates of births and deaths.

Page 33–34
You Spin Me Round (Like a Record) by Dead or Alive
You're No Good by Linda Ronstadt, written by Ballard Clint

Page 36
Description of part of the circulatory system of the body:
Info Bloom, https://www.infobloom.com/how-does-blood-move-through-the-body.htm

Page 40
Darlin You Send Me by Otis Redding
Baby You Can Drive My Car by The Beatles

Page 47
"The whole world is watching"—Chant by protesters at the Democratic National Convention, 1968

JAN WESLEY is the author of *Living in Freefall*, and has two published chapbooks. *Only So Much*, from What Books, is her second full-length poetry book. Poems have appeared in *Askew, Blue Mountain Review, The Iowa Review, Rattle, Spillway, Beyond Words*, and anthologies, among others, and she received a Pushcart nomination. She worked in post-production in the film business for many years, and after receiving an MFA at Vermont College she taught writing at The University of Redlands and The Fashion Institute of Design and Merchandizing. Currently, she facilitates writing workshops in Los Angeles.

WHAT BOOKS PRESS

LOS ANGELES

2022

No One Dies in Palmyra Ohio
HENRY ELIZABETH CHRISTOPHER
NOVEL

Us Clumsy Gods
ASH GOOD
POEMS

Skeletal Lights From Afar
FORREST ROTH
FLASH FICTION/PROSE POEMS

That Blue Trickster Time
AMY UYEMATSU
POEMS

2021

Pyre
MAUREEN ALSOP
POEMS

What Falls Away is Always
HAAKE & WRONSKY, EDITORS
ESSAYS

The Eight Mile Suspended Carnival
REBECCA KUDER
NOVEL

Game
M.L. WILLIAMS
POEMS

2020

No, Don't
ELENA KARINA BYRNE
POEMS

One Strange Country
STELLA HAYES
POEMS

*Remembering Dismembrance:
A Critical Compendium*
DANIEL TAKESHI KRAUSE
NOVEL

Keeping Tahoe Blue
ANDREW TONKAVICH
STORIES

2019

Time Crunch
CATHY COLMAN
POEMS

Whole Night Through
L.I. HENLEY
POEMS

Echo Under Story
KATHERINE SILVER
NOVEL

Decoding Sparrows
MARIANO ZARO
POEMS

2018

Interrupted by the Sea
PAUL LIEBER
POEMS

The Headwaters of Nirvana
BILL MOHR
POEMS

2017

*Gary Oldman Is a Building
You Must Walk Through*
FORREST ROTH
NOVEL

Rhombus and Oval
JESSICA SEQUEIRA
STORIES

Imperfect Pastorals
GAIL WRONSKY
POEMS

2016

The Mysterious Islands
A.W. DEANNUNTIS
STORIES

The "She" Series: A Venice Correspondence
HOLADAY MASON & SARAH MACLAY
POEMS

Mirage Industries
CAROLIE PARKER
POEMS

2015

*The Balloon Containing the Water
Containing the Narrative Begins Leaking*
RICH IVES
STORIES

The Shortest Farewells Are the Best
CHUCK ROSENTHAL & GAIL WRONSKY
LITERARY COLLAGE/PROSE POEMS

2014

It Looks Worse Than I Am
LAURIE BLAUNER
POEMS

They Become Her
REBBECCA BROWN
NOVEL

*The Final Death of Rock-and-Roll
& Other Stories*
A.W. DEANNUNTIS
STORIES

Perfecta
PATTY SEYBURN
POEMS

2013

Brittle Star
ROD VAL MOORE
NOVEL

Sex Libris
JUDITH TAYLOR
POEMS

Start With A Small Guitar
LYNNE THOMPSON
POEMS

Tomorrow You'll Be One of Us
WRONSKY, ROSENTHAL, GRONK
ART/LITERARY COLLAGE/POEMS

2012

The Mermaid at the Americana Arms Motel
A.W. DEANNUNTIS
NOVEL

The Time of Quarantine
KATHARINE HAAKE
NOVEL

Frottage & Even As We Speak
MONA HOUGHTON
NOVELLAS

*West of Eden:
A Life in 21st Century Los Angeles*
CHUCK ROSENTHAL
MAGIC JOURNALISM

2010

Master Siger's Dream
A.W. DEANNUNTIS
NOVEL

Other Countries
RAMÓN GARCÍA
POEMS

A Giant Claw
GRONK
ART
ESSAY BY GAIL WRONSKY
SPANISH TRANSLATION
BY ALICIA PARTNOY

Coyote O'Donohughe's History of Texas
CHUCK ROSENTHAL
NOVEL

So Quick Bright Things
GAIL WRONSKY
POEMS
BILINGUAL, SPANISH TRANSLATION
BY ALICIA PARTNOY

2009

Bling & Fringe (The L.A. Poems)
MOLLY BENDALL & GAIL WRONSKY
POEMS

April, May, and So On
FRANÇOIS CAMOIN
STORIES

One of Those Russian Novels
KEVIN CANTWELL
POEMS

*The Origin of Stars
& Other Stories*
KATHARINE HAAKE
STORIES

Lizard Dream
KAREN KEVORKIAN
POEMS

*Are We Not There Yet? Travels in
Nepal, North India, and Bhutan*
CHUCK ROSENTHAL
MAGIC JOURNALISM

As a small, independent press, we urge our readers to support independent booksellers. This is easily done on our website by purchasing our books either through Indiebound or from BookShop.

WHATBOOKSPRESS.COM

www.ingramcontent.com/pod-product-compliance
Lightning Source LLC
Chambersburg PA
CBHW020545080526
44583CB00013B/999